Perfectly Peculiar Plants

Chris Thorogood

Illustrated by
Catell Ronca

words & pictures

Quarto is the authority on a wide range of topics.
Quarto educates, entertains and enriches the lives of
our readers—enthusiasts and lovers of hands-on living.
www.quartoknows.com

Publisher: Maxime Boucknooghe
Editorial Director: Laura Knowles
Art Director: Susi Martin

Text © Chris Thorogood 2018
Illustrations © Catell Ronca 2018

First published in 2018 by words & pictures,
an imprint of The Quarto Group
6 Orchard Road, Suite 100
Lake Forest, CA 92630
T: +1 949 380 7510
F: +1 949 380 7575
www.QuartoKnows.com

A CIP record for this book is available from the
Library of Congress.

ISBN: 978-1-78603-286-7

Manufactured in Shenzhen, China HH062018

9 8 7 6 5 4 3 2 1

For my niece, Holly, who I hope
will grow to love peculiar plants.
C. T.

To my mum, Catherine, who loved
colors and flowers and who gifted
me her talent.
C. R.

The publishers would like to thank
Richard Mabey for his contribution
to the development of this book.

MIX
Paper from
responsible sources
FSC® C017606
FSC
www.fsc.org

CONTENTS

WHAT'S SO GREAT ABOUT PLANTS?

We depend on plants for our very existence. They produce the oxygen we breathe and the food we eat. Plants are even used to make medicine and clothes!

It's a good thing, then, that plants are such extraordinary survivors. They grow in just about every habitat you can imagine, from frozen arctic cliffs to the driest deserts. They come in all shapes and sizes. Their unique features help them find food, attract pollinators, and spread their seeds.

Fossils show that some of the first flowers looked like magnolias.

Not all plants are as innocent as they look!
Some plants have evolved crafty and unusual
ways to survive. Some have leafy jaws which lie
in wait for unsuspecting insect prey. Others
mimic rotting animal flesh to attract flies.
Some plants even steal their food from the
roots of other plants!

So get ready to discover a world
of perfectly peculiar plants. This
book tells their story...

GIANT WATERLILY
Victoria amazonica

This extraordinary waterlily grows in the warm, shallow waters of the Amazon River. The enormous flat, circular leaves float on the water's surface. They can reach an incredible eight feet across! But not only does the giant waterlily have extraordinary leaves, it also has peculiar flowers...

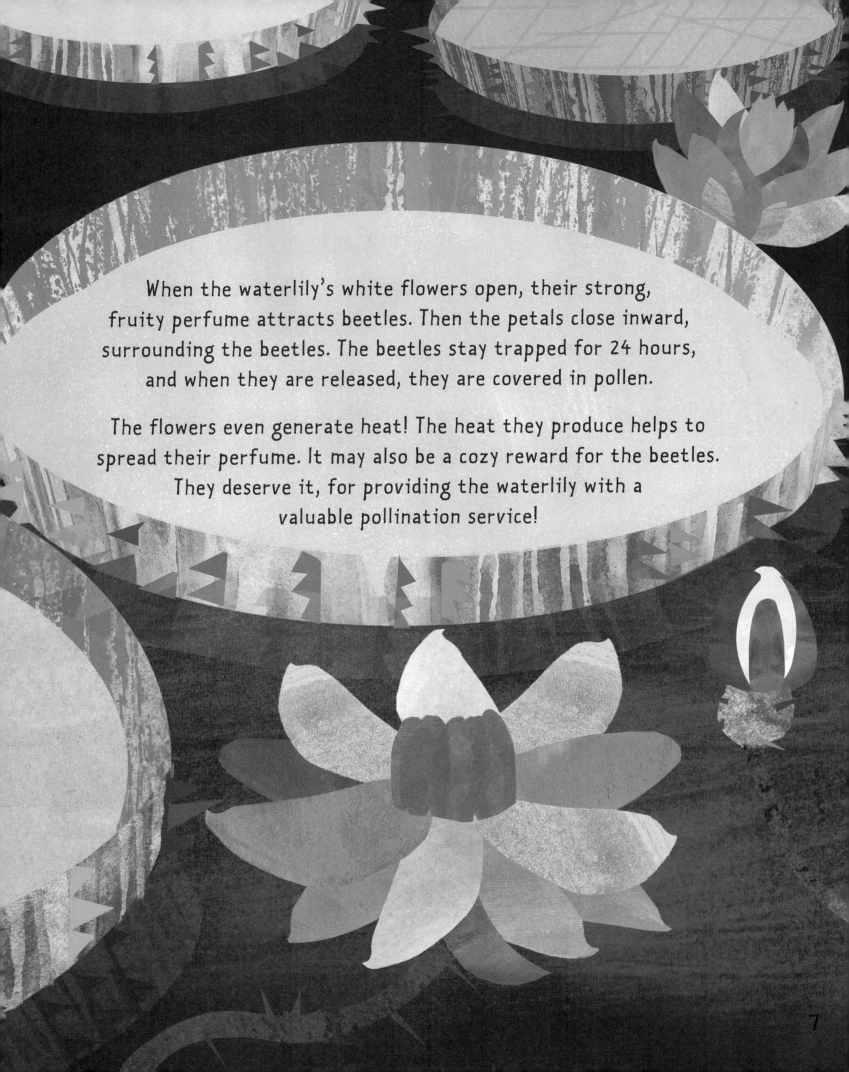

When the waterlily's white flowers open, their strong, fruity perfume attracts beetles. Then the petals close inward, surrounding the beetles. The beetles stay trapped for 24 hours, and when they are released, they are covered in pollen.

The flowers even generate heat! The heat they produce helps to spread their perfume. It may also be a cozy reward for the beetles. They deserve it, for providing the waterlily with a valuable pollination service!

PEBBLE PLANT *Lithops hookeri*

Pebble plants are masters of camouflage found in the deserts of southern Africa. Hungry animals such as tortoises walk straight over what would be a rare meal, mistaking the plant for a pebble!

Because they look so much like stones, they have been called "pebble plants" or "living stones." Their camouflage even includes mottled stripes, lines, and dots, just like the pebbles and stones that surround them.

The fleshy leaves aren't just used for disguise. The plants are succulents, which means they are excellent at storing water.

Plant? What plant?

Most of the pebble plant remains underground, protected from the hot sun. The top of the plant is see-through and acts as a window. It lets in light, which the plant uses to make food.

QUEEN OF THE NIGHT CACTUS

Hylocereus undatus

The queen of the night is a very special cactus. But you have to stay up late to see it! It has very beautiful flowers which open only at night, and close the next morning. They are large, white, and have a strong perfume.

This beautiful cactus is from Central America. It is one of a group of cacti that live perched high in the treetops, or on cliffs. They absorb the nutrients they need from falling leaves and bird droppings. Their thick stems store water and nutrients.

Can you think of another plant that stores water in the same way?

There are several different sorts of queen of the night cactus. Some produce fruits you can eat. The blood-red dragon fruit, for example, is eaten in some parts of the world.

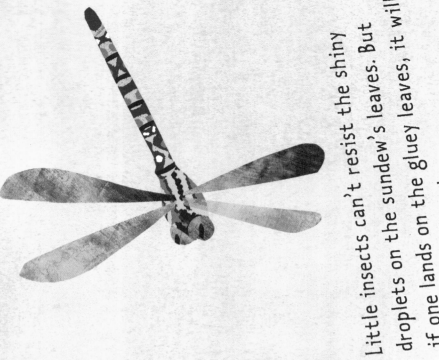

SUNDEW
Drosera rotundifolia

The sundew eats insects—it is a carnivorous plant, like its cousin, the Venus flytrap. It is called a "sundew" because it is covered in tentacles with sticky dew-like droplets.

Little insects can't resist the shiny droplets on the sundew's leaves. But if one lands on the gluey leaves, it will soon become stuck.

The insect panics! The more it tries to escape, the more it gets stuck. After a few minutes, the sundew's tentacles start to bend inward, pinning the insect down.

Eventually the insect is suffocated by the glue. The leaves now make digestive juices—like those in our tummies—to digest them.

sticky glue

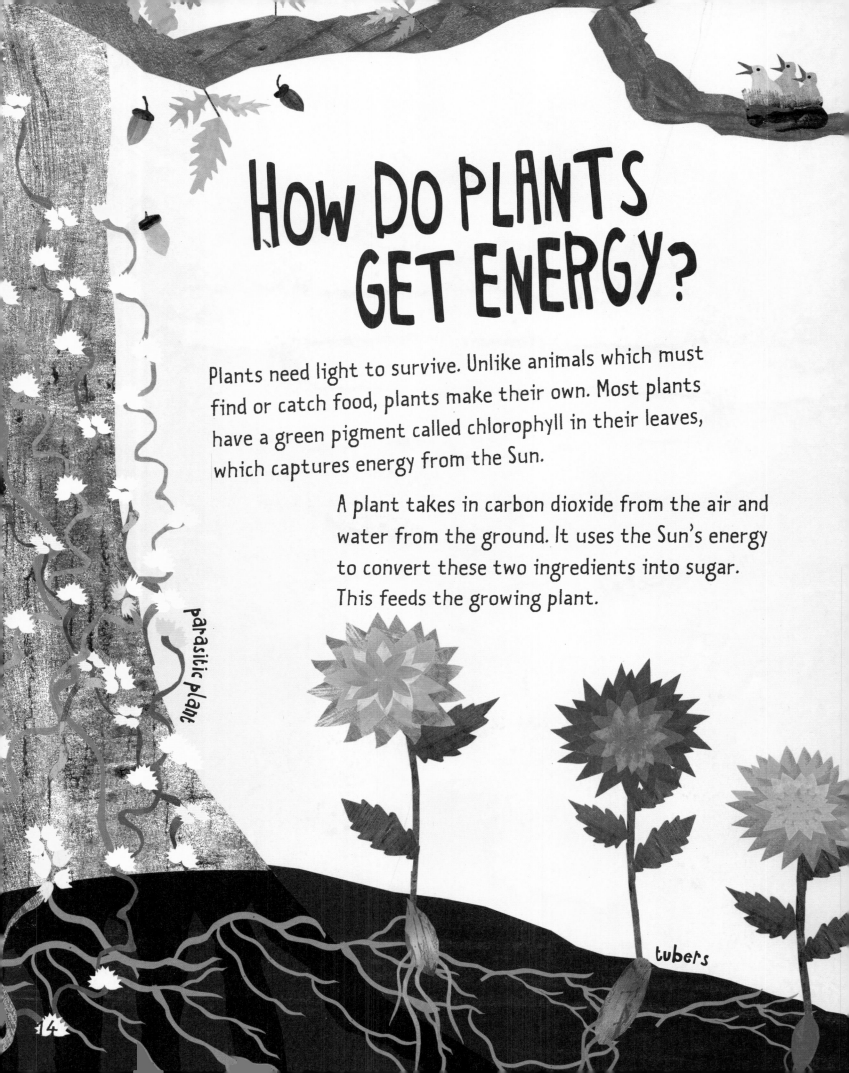

How Do Plants Get Energy?

Plants need light to survive. Unlike animals which must find or catch food, plants make their own. Most plants have a green pigment called chlorophyll in their leaves, which captures energy from the Sun.

A plant takes in carbon dioxide from the air and water from the ground. It uses the Sun's energy to convert these two ingredients into sugar. This feeds the growing plant.

parasitic plant

tubers

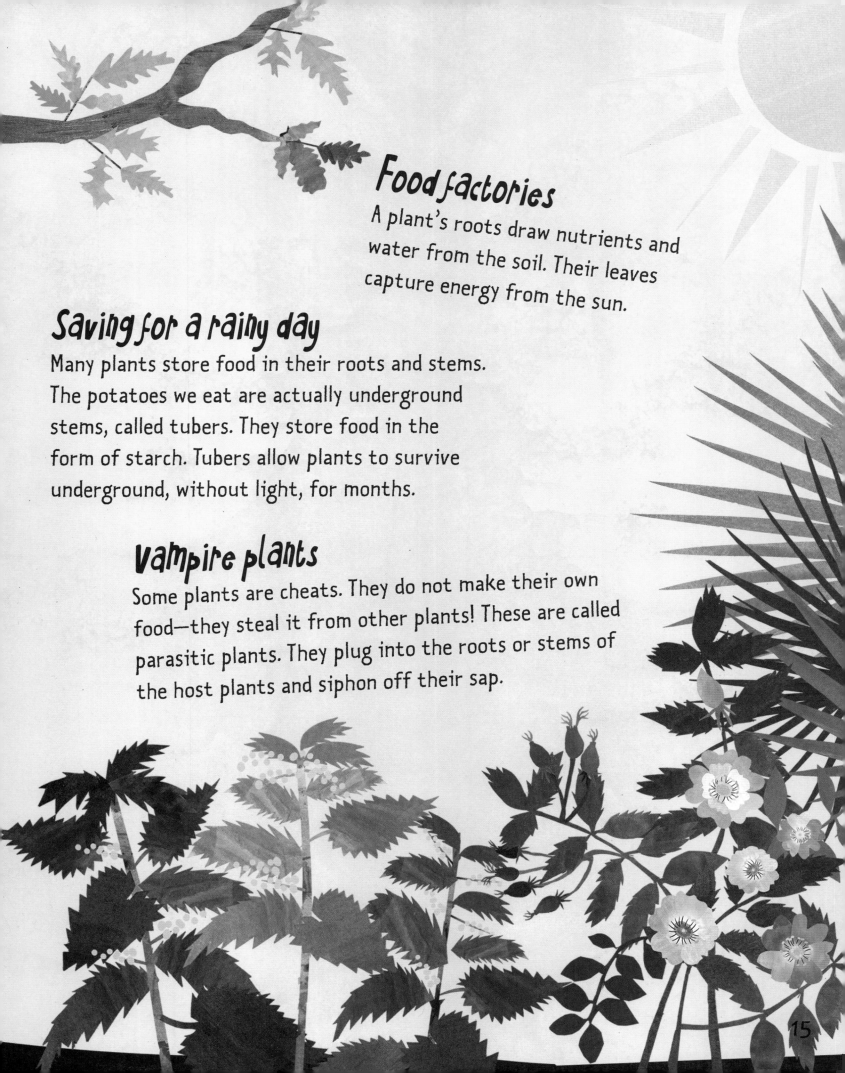

Food factories

A plant's roots draw nutrients and water from the soil. Their leaves capture energy from the sun.

Saving for a rainy day

Many plants store food in their roots and stems. The potatoes we eat are actually underground stems, called tubers. They store food in the form of starch. Tubers allow plants to survive underground, without light, for months.

Vampire plants

Some plants are cheats. They do not make their own food—they steal it from other plants! These are called parasitic plants. They plug into the roots or stems of the host plants and siphon off their sap.

STRANGLER FIG

Ficus benghalensis

The strangler fig is a murderer among plants. Slowly but surely, it actually kills other trees!

The fig begins life high in the branches of a rainforest tree. There is plenty of sunlight up there.

As it grows, it sends down roots which slowly wrap around the trunk of the tree. Once the roots reach the rainforest floor, they take in food from the soil.

The fig grows and grows. Its roots become stronger.

strangling roots

Eventually the fig's victim—the tree inside its roots—may die. But the fig's roots are now so strong that it can stand on its own. It has become a free-standing tree!

Strangler figs are not all bad. They provide a scaffold that can protect other trees from falling during storms.

SAGUARO CACTUS
Carnegiea gigantea

fat, swollen stems

The giant saguaro towers above the other cacti in the North and Central American deserts. Rainstorms are few and far between in the desert, but the saguaro is ready when they arrive! Its roots spread far and wide so it can absorb rainwater quickly. It stores the water in its fat stem.

The saguaro flower opens at night and closes by morning. The flowers are visited by lots of different flying animals including insects, birds, and even bats.

18

flowers

spines

Bats make excellent pollinators. As they bury their heads in the flowers for a drink of sugary nectar, their thick fur picks up lots of pollen.

Thirsty desert animals may want to steal the saguaro's water supply, but they are faced with a prickly problem! A saguaro's stem is covered in sharp spines to protect it.

spines

19

tendril

slippery rim

pool of digestive juices

Inside the pitcher cup, downward-pointing hairs make it impossible for prey to climb back out.

lid to keep out rain

Trapped insects such as ants and termites provide extra nutrients as they are digested by the plant. Drowned rodents have even been found in the traps of one large pitcher plant. Yum!

PITCHER PLANT

Nepenthes rafflesiana

The pitcher plant is a killer plant! It feeds on living things. Creepy-crawlies are attracted to the bright colors and the smell of nectar. But the plant has a cup-shaped trap, called a pitcher. When animals reach the slippery rim, they tumble into the trap, and drown in a pool of digestive liquid at the bottom!

cup-shaped pitcher

Pitcher plants and other carnivorous plants often grow in poor soils, so they have evolved traps to get a juicy meal from the prey they catch.

There are around 150 species of tropical pitcher plant. Most are native to Southeast Asia.

baobab fruits

fat, water-storing trunk

BAOBAB TREE
Adansonia grandidieri

The baobab, also called the "monkey bread tree," is an extraordinary plant. Its giant, swollen trunk stands proud above the savannas of southern Africa and Madagascar.

Like a living reservoir, the water-filled trunk can keep the tree alive through long droughts. In fact, baobab trees are believed to live for over a thousand years!

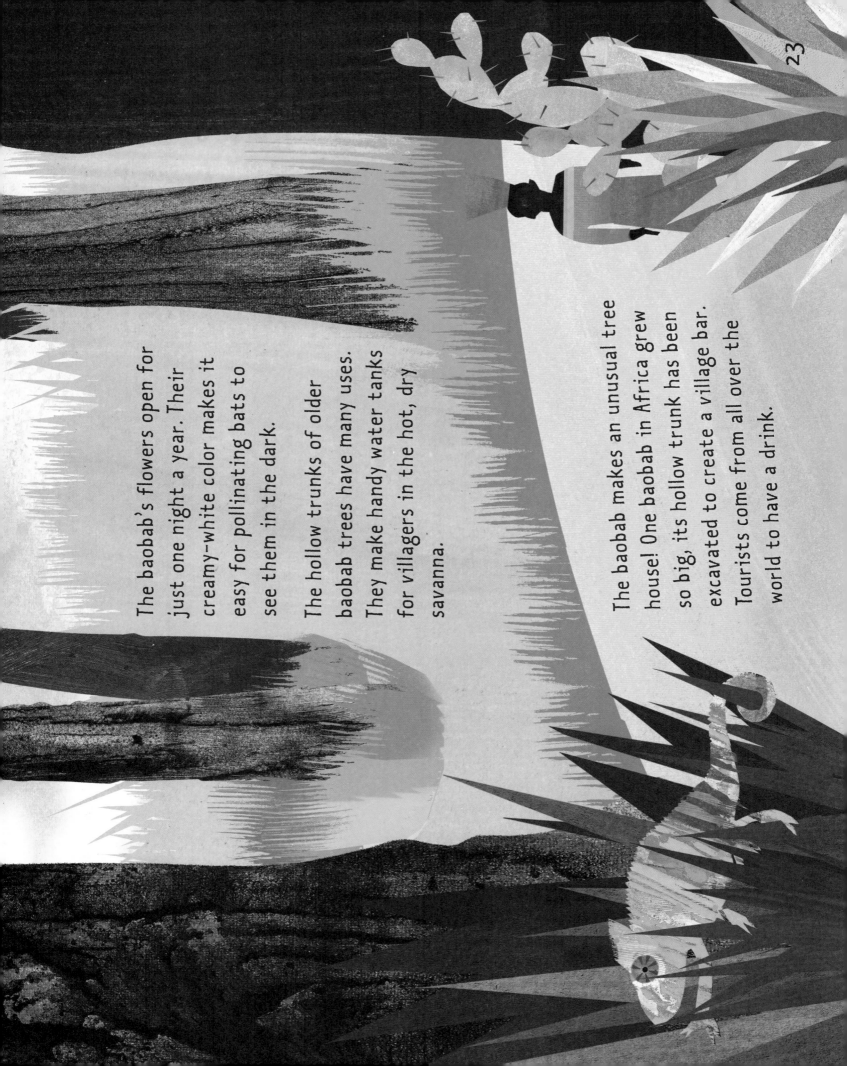

The baobab's flowers open for just one night a year. Their creamy-white color makes it easy for pollinating bats to see them in the dark.

The hollow trunks of older baobab trees have many uses. They make handy water tanks for villagers in the hot, dry savanna.

The baobab makes an unusual tree house! One baobab in Africa grew so big, its hollow trunk has been excavated to create a village bar. Tourists come from all over the world to have a drink.

traveler's palm

LIVING SIDE BY SIDE

Plants have evolved special relationships with lots of different animals. The animals act as messengers, delivering and collecting pollen for the plant. In return, they get a tasty meal—usually a drink of sweet, sugary nectar.

Seeing red

Flowers that attract birds are often red. Hummingbirds can hover in the air, feeding from flowers that other animals cannot reach.

Out of the blue

The traveler's palm grows on Madagascar. On this island there are few birds to disperse its seeds. But the seeds of this plant are bright blue—a color that lemurs love! They eat the blue part and then carry the seeds far and wide.

Night visitors

Flowers which are pollinated by bats and moths are often pale yellow or white. This helps them to stand out in the evening light, when bats and moths come out from their hiding places.

Inseparable

Some plants and animals live together even more closely. Corals may look like a plant, spreading their branches toward the light, but they are actually animals! They do contain tiny plants inside them, called algae. The algae make food from the sun's energy, which feeds the coral. In return, the algae have a safe place to live and lots of light.

coral

ANT PLANT

Hydnophytum formicarum

Ants and plants have lived side by side for 100 million years. Some plants have evolved special relationships with ants. These are called ant plants.

Some ant plants in Southeast Asia and northern Australia grow high in the canopy of the rainforest. Inside their fat stems is a network of hollow passageways and chambers. Ants enter these chambers through holes in the stem. The chambers provide a safe place to raise their young.

swollen stem

It's a tree house for ants!

In return for a nesting place, the ants defend the plants. To protect their home they will viciously attack any animals that try to eat the plant. Some ant colonies even grow fungi inside the ant plants, which they use to feed their young.

Ants have even been seen planting the seeds of the ant plants in little cracks and crevices of tree branches!

TANK BROMELIAD

Aechmea zebrina

Plants need sunlight, but the rainforest floor is a dingy place, where it is difficult for plants to grow. To get around this, tank bromeliads find plenty of sunlight by growing high up in the canopy. They cling on tightly, wrapping their roots around the branches of the tree.

The tank bromeliad's leaves overlap, forming a waterproof tank that collects rainwater. Leaves and bird droppings collect in the bromeliad's leafy pond. These provide food for the plant.

Birds and other animals sip water from the plants. The tank bromeliad is a whole ecosystem, high up in the trees and teeming with life.

Many different types of frog lay their eggs in the tank bromeliad's pond. Their tadpoles feed on insect larvae.

In Jamaica, there is a type of tank bromeliad in which you can even find little land crabs!

overlapping leaves

rainwater-filled pond

Did you know that the pineapple is a kind of bromeliad?

TREE SHREW TOILET PITCHER

Nepenthes lowii

Toilets this way!

Most pitcher plants eat insects, but one pitcher plant in Borneo has evolved a very unusual form of trap. In fact, it hardly catches insects at all. Instead, its sugary nectar attracts something very different—a little furry animal called a tree shrew.

The tree shrews' droppings are a valuable source of nutrients for the plants—just like manure!

The tree shrew climbs onto the pitcher to eat nectar from the lid. While feeding from the lid, the tree shrew's droppings fall straight into the pitcher!

Tree shrew toilet pitchers
evolved this peculiar way
of life high up on remote
mountainsides. Their
relatives in the forests
below eat ants, but there
are few ants higher up
the mountain.

31

BUCKET ORCHID

Coryanthes macrantha

In the rainforests of South America, male bees become very excited when one peculiar orchid—the bucket orchid—comes into flower. This beautiful flower produces a special perfume. The male bees harvest it and use it to attract female bees.

tight passageway

slippery waxy surface

bucket

As the bees crowd around the orchid's strange blooms, one bee falls into its bucket. The bucket is lined with slippery wax. The bee slips and slides, and cannot climb out.

He panics, and finds the only escape route: a tight passageway at the back of the bucket which he has to squeeze through.

As he slowly wriggles his way out, a big dollop of pollen is glued to his back.

If the bee falls into another bucket orchid, he will deliver his cargo of pollen and pollinate the flower.

It's an orchid obstacle course!

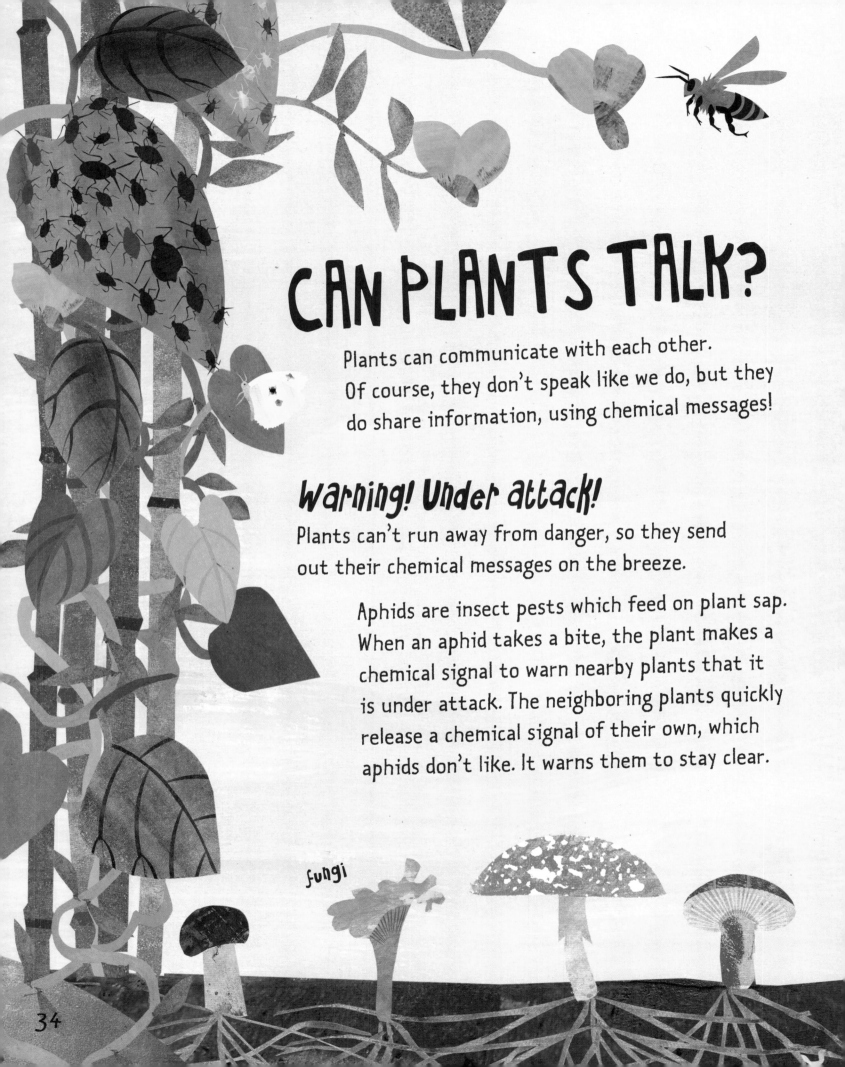

CAN PLANTS TALK?

Plants can communicate with each other. Of course, they don't speak like we do, but they do share information, using chemical messages!

Warning! Under attack!

Plants can't run away from danger, so they send out their chemical messages on the breeze.

Aphids are insect pests which feed on plant sap. When an aphid takes a bite, the plant makes a chemical signal to warn nearby plants that it is under attack. The neighboring plants quickly release a chemical signal of their own, which aphids don't like. It warns them to stay clear.

fungi

Stink-mail

Some of the messages that plants send out are loud and clear! The durian fruit attracts lots of rainforest animals with its strange, unpleasant aroma. It smells like a blocked drain!

Orangutans find the custard-like flesh very tasty. They swallow the seeds, which eventually pass through in their droppings.

durian fruit

Rumouring roots

Fungi have tiny, hair-like threads which wrap around the roots of many plants. These connections let the plant and fungus exchange food. Plants can also use these fungal threads like underground telephone wires, sharing messages with each other. They warn each other that insects are on the attack!

35

Mopane trees are common on the hot, dry grasslands of southern Africa. Elephants absolutely love their leaves, and will tear off whole branches to get their daily ration. But the trees have a secret weapon. They "talk" to each other, warning neighboring trees to defend themselves.

When the mopane leaves are munched, they release a chemical signal into the air.

This chemical drifts on the wind. When it reaches the leaves of neighboring trees, it makes them produce nasty-tasting chemicals called tannins, which the elephants hate.

The elephants are clever players in this game too. Some of them may have learned to forage against the wind, so that the chemical signal is blown away from the trees they're heading toward.

Mopane seeds are popular local snacks.

MOPANE

Colophospermum mopane mopane mopane

Flies crawl into a chamber and become trapped by downward-pointing spines. Overnight, the plant showers the flies with pollen. The next day, the spines wither, and the flies are released to visit another plant.

spike-like spadix

prison chamber

38

DEAD HORSE ARUM

Helicodiceros muscivorus

Here is a plant which both looks and smells like a rotting animal. It grows on Mediterranean clifftops which are home to flocks of seagulls. The cliffs are smelly places with droppings everywhere—a perfect place for flies. The dead horse arum makes a smell almost *identical* to that of a rotting gull. Nice!

hairy surface

The dead horse arum's blooms are even covered in hair, just like fur or mold on a dead animal.

BEE ORCHID
Ophrys apifera

With their wing-like petals, furry bodies, and stubby antennae, the flowers of bee orchids look like little multicolored bumblebees on stalks. But why would a flower have evolved to look like an insect?

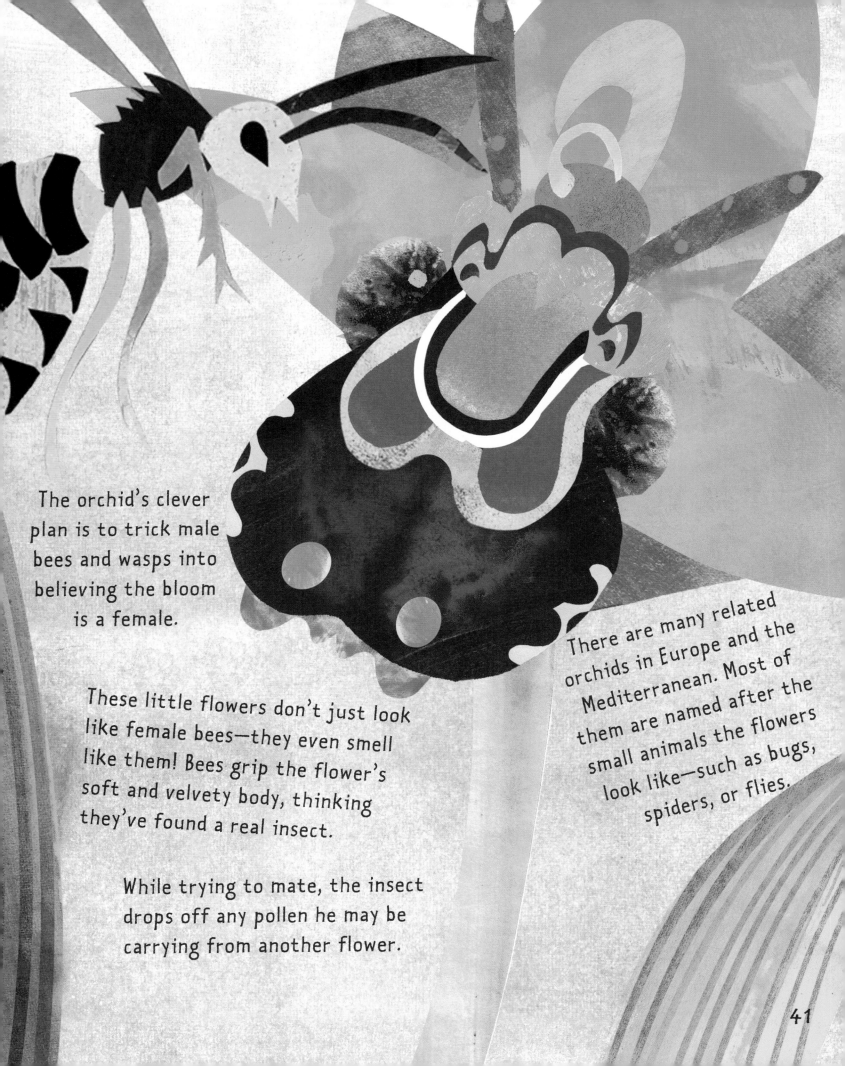

The orchid's clever plan is to trick male bees and wasps into believing the bloom is a female.

These little flowers don't just look like female bees—they even smell like them! Bees grip the flower's soft and velvety body, thinking they've found a real insect.

While trying to mate, the insect drops off any pollen he may be carrying from another flower.

There are many related orchids in Europe and the Mediterranean. Most of them are named after the small animals the flowers look like—such as bugs, spiders, or flies.

RAFFLESIA
Rafflesia arnoldii

Imagine their surprise when explorers first found this monster of a plant! Rafflesia is the world's largest flower, measuring up to five feet across. There are about 30 different types of rafflesia. The largest grows in the rainforests of Sumatra and Borneo, and is very rare.

Rafflesia has no green leaves and no roots. It cannot make its own food, so it steals water and nutrients from the roots of tropical vines. It is a vampire plant!

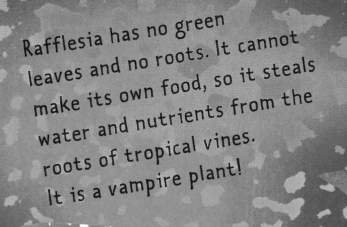

Rafflesia rarely flowers and is almost impossible to grow. Few people are lucky enough to see it.

Rafflesia smells like rotting flesh—what a stinker! The huge flower spreads the awful smell far and wide to attract pollinating flies from across the rainforest.

Can you think of another flower that smells horrible in order to attract flies?

43

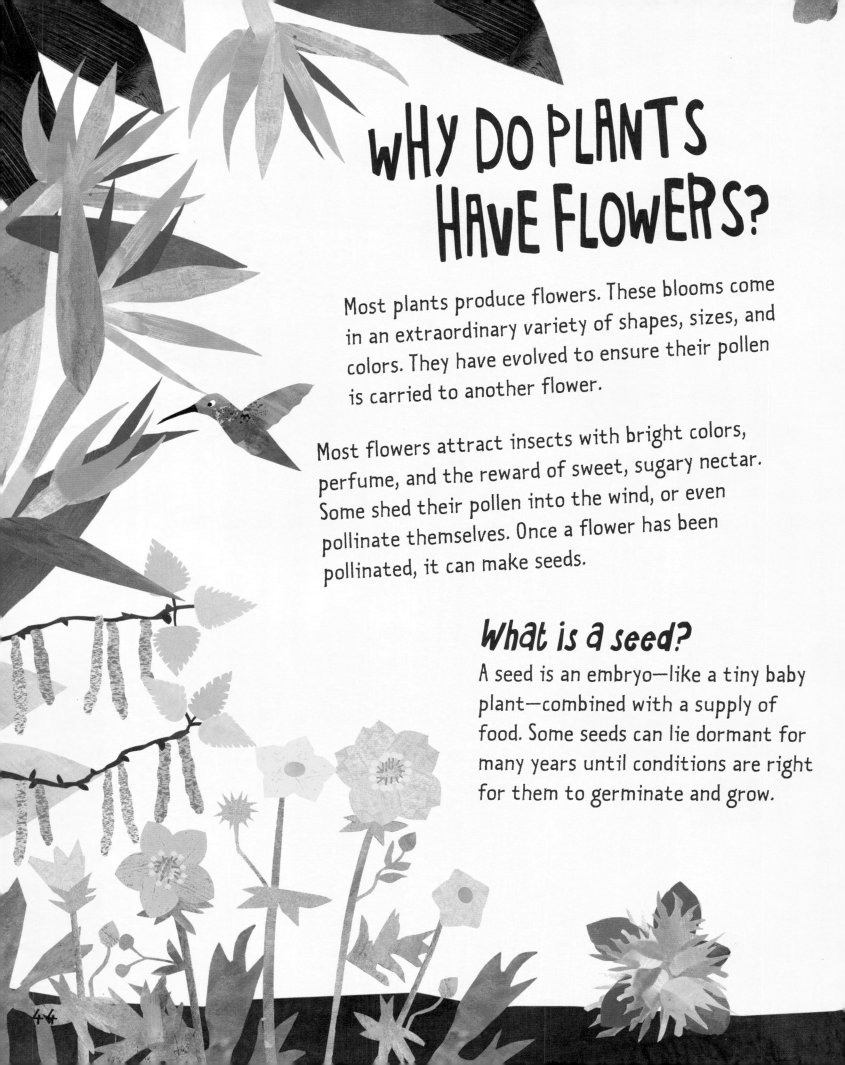

WHY DO PLANTS HAVE FLOWERS?

Most plants produce flowers. These blooms come in an extraordinary variety of shapes, sizes, and colors. They have evolved to ensure their pollen is carried to another flower.

Most flowers attract insects with bright colors, perfume, and the reward of sweet, sugary nectar. Some shed their pollen into the wind, or even pollinate themselves. Once a flower has been pollinated, it can make seeds.

What is a seed?

A seed is an embryo—like a tiny baby plant—combined with a supply of food. Some seeds can lie dormant for many years until conditions are right for them to germinate and grow.

Strange but true

The tiny flowers of the fig are hidden away inside the fruit. Wasps climb into the fig and lay their eggs, dropping off pollen at the same time. Once the grubs become grown-up wasps they bite their way out and fly off in search of a new fig to lay their eggs in. The plant needs the wasps to make seeds.

fig plant

Cheats!

A few flowers—including many orchids—trick insects into pollinating them without offering any reward at all. Some flowers even pretend to be a rotting animal to attract pollinating flies.

No flower? No problem!

Some plants, such as mosses and ferns, do not produce flowers or seeds. They are known as primitive plants, and they reproduce by tiny dust-like spores which are carried away by wind and water.

Other non-flowering plants include the conifers, which produce seeds inside special structures called cones. Christmas trees are conifers!

orchid

cones

45

sticky hooks

flower

BURDOCK
Arctium lappa

This clever plant inspired the idea behind Velcro—the sticky material we use to fasten our shoes. In 1941, a Swiss engineer discovered that his dog's fur was covered in burrs—the seeds of the burdock plant. He looked at the burrs under a microscope and discovered that they had tiny hooks which catch onto hair and fabric.

Burdocks are common in Europe, where they can be found growing along riverbanks and in woods.

The reason the burdock produces such sticky seeds is simple: they cling on to the fur of passing animals. When the seeds eventually fall on the ground, they have found a new place to grow.

Animals provide a free delivery service for the plant, spreading the seeds far and wide!

TITAN ARUM
Amorphophallus titanum

The titan arum is a huge tropical plant. In the wild it grows only on the island of Sumatra, in Southeast Asia. Its giant yellow flower spike—called a spadix—is the biggest in the plant world. It can reach a whopping eight feet tall! But the titan arum's real claim to fame is that it is one of the nastiest smelling plants on the planet.

When the titan arum blooms, thousands of tiny flowers burst open at the bottom of the spike. The spike makes a horrendous stench. This attracts the sort of little flies that feed on dead meat. The flies think they have found a tasty meal and crawl all over the flowers, picking up pollen as they go.

The titan arum takes many years to flower, but in the last week before it opens, the flower bud can grow up to an incredible three inches per day.

SEA BEAN

Entada gigas

This incredible little bean travels farther than any other plant. Its seeds hang from vines in giant pods. These vines grow many miles from the sea, in hot places in Africa, Australia, and South America.

When the pods are ripe, they fall from the plant into the river below. As the pods float away, they split open and release lots of large, brown, floating seeds.

seed pod

Eventually the seeds reach the sea.
They may travel across the sea's
surface for thousands of miles.
Some may even reach the cold sandy
beaches of Great Britain, to be
picked up by curious vacationers!

If the sea bean reaches a warm,
sandy beach or riverbank,
it may germinate—even if it
is many miles from where its
journey began.

seafaring seeds

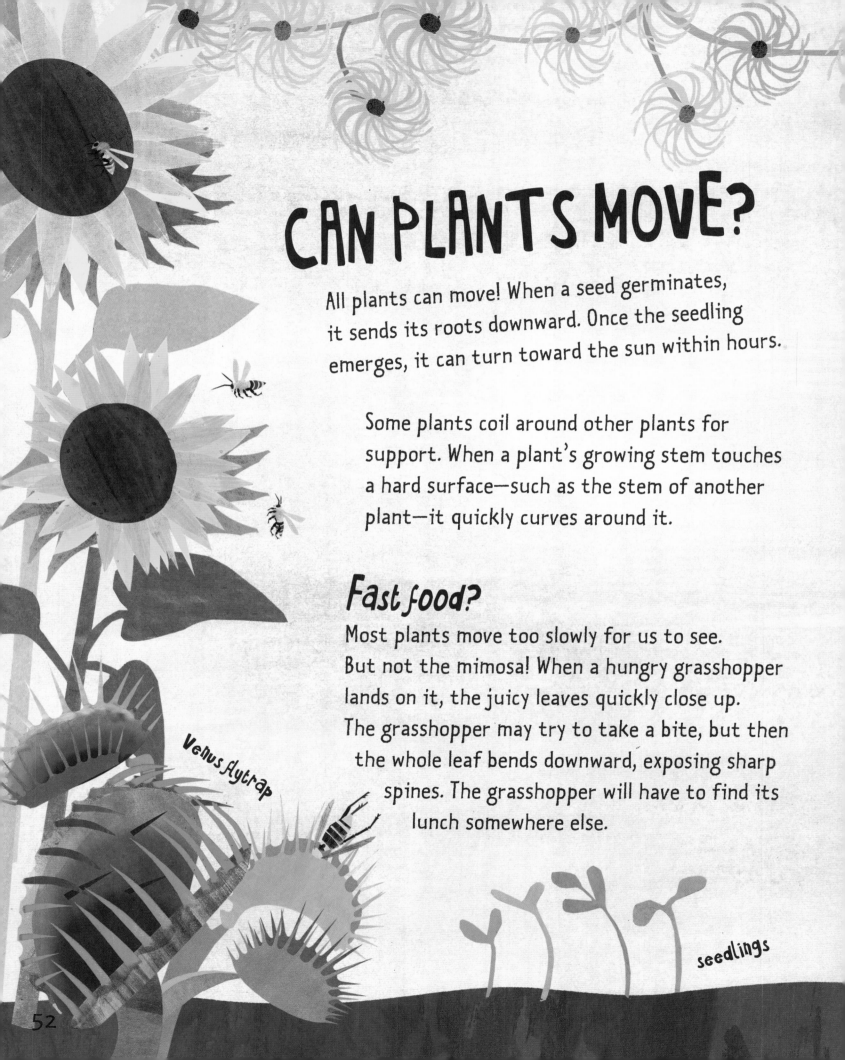

CAN PLANTS MOVE?

All plants can move! When a seed germinates, it sends its roots downward. Once the seedling emerges, it can turn toward the sun within hours.

Some plants coil around other plants for support. When a plant's growing stem touches a hard surface—such as the stem of another plant—it quickly curves around it.

Fast food?

Most plants move too slowly for us to see. But not the mimosa! When a hungry grasshopper lands on it, the juicy leaves quickly close up. The grasshopper may try to take a bite, but then the whole leaf bends downward, exposing sharp spines. The grasshopper will have to find its lunch somewhere else.

Venus flytrap

seedlings

mimosa

Castaways and skydivers

Seeds must move to spread far and wide. Some plants' seeds catch a ride on the wind or the water. Even very large seeds can find a new home this way!

Coconuts fall from a tree and float on the ocean currents. They may wash up on a beach many miles away. If they find a warm, damp, sandy spot, they will quickly germinate and grow into a new coconut tree.

Milkweed seeds are much lighter. Each has a tiny, silky parachute. When the milkweed's pods are ripe, they burst open, releasing their seeds into the wind.

vENUS FLYTRAP

Dionaea muscipula

The Venus flytrap is a plant predator. Its leafy jaws lie in wait for insect prey. If an insect crawls onto the surface, then... *snap!* The trap is sprung! The unsuspecting insect is caught in a leafy snare.

This clever little plant can do more than just eat insects—it can count! If an insect touches the little hairs on its surface once, the jaws remain open. Touch them again, and the jaws snap shut. This stops the plant from wasting energy trapping falling leaves that may land on it.

Look out! It's a trap!

Can you think of another plant that feeds on insects?

As the insect wriggles inside the trap, the plant releases digestive juices, like those we make in our own tummies. These break down the insect, releasing nutrients for the hungry plant.

Once the Venus flytrap has digested its meal, the jaws spring open again. All that remains of the insect is its dry skeleton. The plant is ready for its next victim...

trigger hairs

SQUIRTING CUCUMBER

Ecballium elaterium

This isn't an ordinary cucumber. It certainly isn't a cucumber you can eat. This is a *squirting* cucumber.

Look out! It's about to explode!

The squirting cucumber grows in dry places in the Mediterranean. It has hairy leaves and little yellow flowers.

In summer, it produces bristly fruits on long stalks. When the fruits are ripe, they fill with liquid. They get so full that the slightest touch makes them explode!

Can you think of another plant that can move quickly when touched?

The cucumber is hurled high into the air. As it goes, it sends out a jet of water, full of seeds. The seeds are spread far and wide, allowing the plant to find new places to grow.

seeds

fruits

flowers

RESURRECTION PLANT

Selaginella lepidophylla

The resurrection plant belongs
to a very ancient group of plants.
It is an incredible desert survivor that can
survive for years without any rainwater at all.

Can you think of another plant that can survive with very little water?

The resurrection plant grows in the hot, dry deserts of Mexico and North America. During dry weather, the plant's spiraled stems curl up into a nest-like ball. It may remain this way for years—brown and crispy, like a ball of dead leaves. This protects the sensitive middle part of the plant from the hot desert sun.

When the rain eventually arrives, the resurrection plant quickly springs to life. It uncurls its stems and turns green within just a few hours. It grows throughout the rainy season. When the desert dries up again, it closes back up into a lifeless ball.

You can grow a resurrection plant yourself. Place it in a saucer of water on a windowsill and watch it unfurl and turn green!

AIR PLANT

Tillandsia pretiosa

Air plants live high in the forest canopy, where they hang from the branches of trees. There are hundreds of different types of air plant. Most of them live in the forests of North, South, and Central America.

The seeds of the air plant are covered in long hairs. The hairs act as a parachute, carrying them far and wide on the wind.

Air plants have no roots to absorb nutrients from the soil. Instead, they absorb water and nutrients directly from the air.

Dust and minerals in the air dissolve into rainwater and dew. This water is absorbed by tiny hairs on the air plant's leaves. The hairs also capture minerals washed off the bark of the host tree.

PROTECTING PLANTS

When you hear "endangered," you may think of pandas or rhinos, but plants can be endangered too. This means there are not many of them left in the wild. Without protection, they may go extinct.

Plants face many threats. Their habitat can be destroyed to make way for buildings or farmland. Rare plants might be illegally collected from the wild, or other plants and animals might take over their habitat.

The golf ball cactus grows in the mountains of Mexico. It has been illegally collected to be sold as a houseplant. Sadly, most of the wild golf ball cacti are now gone.

The gold of Kinabalu orchid grows in only one place: Mount Kinabalu on the island of Borneo. Some people will pay thousands of dollars for just one stem of its cut flowers. Thankfully, the orchid is now protected in the wild.

In South America, thick rainforests provide a home for many different plants and animals. But large areas of rainforest have been cut down—and lost forever—to make way for growing crops.

People depend on plants. Plants provide food, and many important medicines can be made from plants. However, people are also the biggest threat to plants today. If we want to survive, we must protect plants and their habitats, all around the world.

Plants can be useful or poisonous, pretty or peculiar, but they all deserve a place on planet Earth.

gold of Kinabalu orchid

golf ball cacti

INDEX